Now in a Far Sky

Now in a Far Sky

Sharon Darrow

Vermont Poems

Pudding Hill Press
Sutton, Vermont

Copyright © 2019 by **Sharon Darrow**

All rights reserved. No part of this publication may be reproduced, distributed or transmitted in any form or by any means, without prior written permission.

Pudding Hill Press
5463 Pudding Hill
Sutton, Vermont 05867
www.sharondarrow.com

Now in a Far Sky/ Sharon Darrow. -- 1st ed.
978-0-9986878-3-4

For Jerry

Frail sentence moved by/ the seismic sway of existence

–ROCKS ON A PLATTER, BARBARA GUEST

Contents

voice lessons 1
dream 2
voice of silence   wind   stone 4
blue snow lasts in the memory 8
sunlight shifts   green 10
preserve this moment: 12
o taste & see 14
dark fin 16
now in a far   sky 22
what is 28
morning   visitation 30
Sun after Snow 31
Lark of Larches 32
Final 35
Song for the Slow Winter 36
sunlight on branches 38
I came upon a hill and as a dream 39
I am made of earth and water 40

voice lessons

  when the self of   myself

      tongues the heart of   myself

           language awakens   births voice

  when heart's language   thaws

      our frozen tongues   our voices

           rise   speak   our own stories

  thrill to our deep   hidden harmonies

      our voices   cannot be unheard

           our songs   unsung

dream

    I awake abuzz with light

        beating wings of light

            golden honey light!   beehive

    honey-combed   translucent

        bright   I am queen

            I am worker and drone

    honey and comb   all me

        drawn to flowers   deep

            petals   stamens   pollen

    covers my shoulders   I fly

        home   feed myself

            upon my own throne

birth selves of myself

      pour into each   golden

            honey   warm   sudden

feast   blessed sunlight

      I fly   dance the journey's

            map drawn upon blank air

marked indelible on invisible

      light   shining dust motes

            lifted by breeze   beckon

all my selves to follow

      on wings of summer

            blue   creation of light

voice of silence   wind   stone

1. voice of silence:

       hush, little baby,

       don't you…

       shhh…no, don't

       you…   i am silence

thrum of blood   narrowed

arteries behind your eyes

                silence

       don't you cry

unless in silence

              don't tell about…shhh

       don't mention…shhh

cry out in silence

        only the voice of stone

                echoes   through these canyons

2. voice of wind:

        violence is my name

        kind as a lamb

        hurricane of joy

        tornado of mourning

hollow shriek in your ears

concrete canyons sizzle in blue neon

    lightning   my daughter

    hail   my only son

who has seen the wind   who

    howls like i howl who streams

through your body   your prayers

        hand to hand   into the air

3. voice of stone:

        deep sounds

    strain at the belt of night, duende

    inhabits the soul of stone, cold

    hard granite night, everlasting

    my crystalline heart beats

    slow as one turn round the sun

    stillness speaks one syllable

    each million years, wind-scudded

    boulder in the dry river bed, wind-

    shaven skin smooth as silence

    wind-broken sands scatter,

    fall, fill the mouth of silence

    stones cry out, wind rains

    light into your mouth,

    breaks your stony silence

blue snow lasts in the memory

late snowfall creeps low
        on the heels of an early green blade peeking
        at doe and fawn just in time   grass warms
a last fringe of snow   lacy ice

mud drags its hem across
        meadow night   moonshadows wake
        silent and chilled furry sleepers
creepers across the forest's first leaves

incredible as stars   shivering in blue dawn
        after the lash of storm and starving

        new grasses already raising
fur into seed and sift   solemn feast
meant to save the lonely wanderer
        near a crossroad of faith afraid

       to speak of what cannot

arrive   to mouth the words

"who will not take the early road

       sail the late tide   brave the towering

       cloud   who will not go with rain

or laughing bolt of light

this third half of night?"

       spring's mystery longs to unveil

       as blue cloth sewn over a doorway   sealed only once

blue winds   brittle

color of sky at brilliance in ice   cold

       blue   glass raised to drink to winter's ending

       blue light on blue water   dance of smooth round

stones   a cool blue breeze grazes the upheld wrist

sunlight shifts   green

    boughs sway   tangled

    days fly   away

    limbs   needles

    catch fall sting

    skin dappled dark

    sorrows rise

        dawn-light dandelions

        flee away   carry

        tonnage of star-loss

        shiver   tasseled

        bright   bloom

        soon gone

froth-white   blown

stars   flow away

fountaining   sun

skyward   and   down

fast   earthborn

breeze on skin

preserve this moment:

1.

tiny leaf hangs by a strand to its mother plant
twists in the light   dim then bright

untended perennial garden at full growth
height of summer

northernmost sunsets
this heat

on a green lawn   old cats'
new feet

so much water
we will never thirst again

blessings of   crabapple   winter
promise for deer

a lonely dog barks—once—distant
grumbling in the clouds   fades   sound

felt more than heard   fades   rises
                                        fades

2.

a tractor's steady hum   harvests
end-of-summer hay

beyond seven ridges   horizon
smudged with softness   day's gradual turning

away from dawn passing into clouds   rain
sounding its tap-tap music into night

late clear sky   star strewn   moonless
not lonely   shared in silence

search the brown-red apple skin   mottled yellow
pattern of autumn's first leaf

amid the still green   so green summer
find in that shape-taste the quench of yearning

grown so old   too long and too late
bird chirp   insect tinnitus rattle

o taste & see

        the world is

                fruit, not beholden to

    anyone

      taste   flowering plum

flood on river stone   trance

      robin's hobbly-bobbly

    weave of worm & tilt-

          eye up, now down

the world is with us today

                blue, its cool

fire rains dawn upon our heads

       vanguard   locus

      old seashells   &   pine cones

      smell of pitch dust

   yellow holes in the wood-tapped

           pine beside little

               hat-stacked fungi

children ride ponies, their voices

          music, the hooves clip-

                 clop the rhythm

dark fin

1.

                    skims my toes

        brook pool bright with stones

      sunlight   swims its speckled way

                below the watery horizon

            cool as sin

2.

                hot to the core   my eyes

        pencil sketch the beech's

   limp leaves   lose focus

       beyond white   deep into blue

              mere vastness

                                      brightening

3.

                                        breeze on damp

        skin   a riddle   a frog

                  prize of nightfall   fireflies rise

            grass to trees   rove

                      forest's edge

                              little fiddlers scratch out

              tunes   secret rhizomes

      plan to bloom   clouds'

            slow   passage over   our valley

blows away the last stars

distant   thunderstorms

fetch light

4.

        ghost car   one blue sound

                                                                               disappears

at mid-bridge

                      long forgotten   wreckage

            past's   dear disguise

                                beyond the hedge a ridge

5.
                dog's shallow bark

heat   lightning flash   flaps   its billowy   sheet

           pink tent   arches   over the high meadow

                      frightening a lark   alone

               pecking at
                                    mites
  on her wing

now in a far   sky

       mountains

              green wind

              leaves inside out

                        changes blowing

        across the valley

a dairy farm: two arched

barns   two old brick

one tall white house

a sign

       take back

vermont

brings an august chill   but fine sun

    on late blooms

what is meant by a bell

when the sky clears enough to hear it

when your open lips taste its one note

what is meant by one flame

a candle in the twilight pale as the sun

what is meant by this ripe black raspberry this one ripe berry

what is meant by the caw & coo

timid step of the fawn sent out alone at dusk

antlers just beginning to sprout

forty turkeys on the road

what is meant by two red foxes & a coyote's howl

peeling paper bark of the white white birch

dying larch, brown in midsummer

when water flows over stones we are made one with it

molecule for molecule, ion for ion and we dream:

    berries & sweet cream plenty

    joy from one's own beating heart

        full breath

        dancing feet

what is meant by this woman

beyond her own ability to imagine

what is meant   by this woman   sitting alone

content in the kindly breeze in the safe sunlight

in this place of her own

    blow across the valley   wind   fly but not

    in a dream of flying   blow each cloud

        each snag of twig & twist of bone

        know faith   go with the wind

            blow across sky

cover the feet of birds

cover the hands of the worried

cover the eyes of the sorrowful

                & speak stillness

what is this for   this life of my own

where have my children grown

                    grow   like a hardy plant

roots   stems   buds   flowers fruit   seeds

        grow

myself into green

                crabapple bittersweet maple

                    oak ash cedar lilac apple

                        peach pear apricot grape

                                o vine & vine & vine

what is

true?	color
this leaf	holds
without	sunshine

water or chlorophyll—	
red orange	yellow—
fills eyes	breath

opens	longing
satisfies this	moment
this color	is

true	darkness
opens to	night
day-blind	eyes

search	deep blue
color	that is
true	what is

a star?	heat
gravity	or dust
from these	eyes

shaken from	hands
opened for	bright
leaf-fall	alight

a million	billion
light-	years traversed
alone	for this

truth: suns   die
blazing   birth dust
motes' shine-   drift

across my   window
this   one more
autumn-orange   sunset

lamps lit   bright
house spinning   under
life's last   star

morning visitation

conifers' shivery branches
        brushy boughs
tiny   black and white birds

deciduous trunks lean   askew
       strike long notes
between dark   green and gray-

white sky held up by snow-   sheltered
high meadow
a dozen years   gone

memory foxes bark   cavort
in moonlight
              laugh/sing   in dream-light

touched by a distant feather of cloud
    early light
moves far mountains   near

Sun after Snow

Not from clouds but branches,
snow sifts from limbs

slanted through pines.
A breeze now, sun rising.

Sugar snow sifts from limbs,
glints on snow banks.

A breeze now, sun risen,
blue shadows scatter

glitter on snow banks.
Wind blows, rains down

blue shadows, scatters
snowflakes, whirls blue sky.

Wind-snow rains down,
shakes out early sunlight.

Snow whirls from blue sky's
stirring, snowflakes fall,

shiver through early light
slanted through pines.

Stirring, snowflakes fall,
not from clouds but branches

Lark of Larches

(after Edna St. Vincent Millay's "Counting-Out Rhyme")

I.

Slivered dark reaches my pillow,

Dark and shallow searching fellow.

Branch of aloe

Lash in crimson, harshlit gable

Stain and ransom, grievous fable.

Darkling cobble,

Lightning cobble, smooth as moongleam

Lightning stroke, its joke a gone-gleam

Light, a torn gleam,

Sliver darkling reach and follow,

Limb of ancient golden fellow,

Branch of aloe.

II.

Winter lark of snow, and terror

    lark of shadow trill and mirror

        twist of air or

glance of chill on deer-moon birches,

    tree or hill instead of churches,

        Lark of Larches.

Moon of larches poor as snow-shine,

    moon of rime for rhyme and starshine,

        moon of lark-shine.

Winter lark of ice, and eros'

    lash of frost-fire, silvered mirrors,

        twisted arrows.

III.

Water rocky deep, and rippled
Raucous purple dawn and purple
Twilight circle.

Dash of orange in sky-brook color,
Sunset torn from worn out cloudburst,
Rock of amber.

Brook of summer, full of rushes,
Brook of spring flood glows in fall flush,
Brook of snow-hush.

Water rocky deep, and stippled
Shadow fishes, gold and purple
Twilit circle.

Final

(after Roethke)

The town's last restaurant
closes its doors, a winter ruin;

mud season takes its toll
upon the eye and rock and cloud,

red leather left to cool,
last cut of meat devoured

by hermits in the wavering,
who hug sharp objects left at rest

to curve with pleasure toward the last
upturned chair and pause to say

ghosts have gathered up their cares
and washed the dishes of the stars:

To cut the cord of winters' past,
to ruin summer's last green hill,

to speak of life as of decay,
a dog, the slag, a pure belief,

relief of blue, an honest season,
reason enough to leave off leaving.

Song for the Slow Winter

(after Wallace Stevens)

In fire, near the light,
The song in the coasts
And on the risen seas,
Scouring itself,
Falling on this moon,
For the sea itself
Fallen on the air.
See: yet the song for the slow winter
Rose beckoning
And I sought the patience in the hunter.

The hollows in the days
Were as the sea itself
Falling on the air
On the lengthening air.
They dove under the moon,
Near as it sighed in the arms of the winter
Far from the earth.
I saw its patience--the winter.
Was it patient beyond the lengthening
or beyond the sea itself
Pealing on the air,
Paling as the twilight
Impaled on light
Falling like the day of the hunter
Fallen on the proud light,
Proud as the winter
Distant in the patience of the hunter?
Or was it patient beyond the winter?

Inside the hearth,
I hear now a vision rendered
As a sea itself
Falling on the air.
I hear now the colors rush,
Rise beckoning as a chant for the slow winter
I lean alone.
And I enter the patience of the hunter.

sunlight on branches

(with lines from Rumi's "Zero Circle")

across the road   seen through
evergreen boughs   striped

blotched   shredded light—
I am *helpless before it,*

dumbfounded by its torn
wintered beauty   snow

mound in foreground stabbed
with straw-tasseled sticks   old

weeds   summer-dead
I am *unable to say yes or no*

stricken in awe of light
of new snow   of old cloud

pastel sheen shimmering
pink to peach under the cedars

I came upon a hill and as a dream

this hill rose into darkness

star-strewn   wind-wild

made for song   for chill

breath   to inhale night

exhale stars   whole galaxies

a universe   boundless

enough for all this

all sorrows   joys   songs

my open mouth breathes

midnight's wild   chill wind

I am made of earth and water

    lost   inside   my dreams

                  lighted candles in your windows

        call me back   to waking

    lost inside   my dreams

        asleep   bees bomb and strafe

          call me   back to waking

                lead me down an open path

       sleep bees   bomb and strafe

           my closing eyes   lost visions

lead me down the open path

      where I'm from   where I'm going

        my closing eyes' lost visions

   light the candles in our windows

where I'm going   where I'm from

About the Author

Sharon Darrow was on the faculty of Vermont College of Fine Arts for over 20 years. She is the award-winning author of fiction and poetry for children and young adults. Her poems, short stories, interviews, and personal essays for adults have appeared in literary journals *Rhino, Folio, Whetstone, ACM (Another Chicago Magazine), Columbia Poetry Review, Great River Review, Other Voices, The Writer's Chronicle,* and in the anthology, *In the Middle of the Middle West,* Her most recent book for adults is *Worlds within Words: Writing and the Writing Life.* The Darrow Lecture Series, named in her honor, is held annually in Montpelier, Vermont, with lectures delivered by distinguished authors who are graduates of the MFA in Writing for Children and Young Adults program.

www.ingramcontent.com/pod-product-compliance
Lightning Source LLC
Chambersburg PA
CBHW050448010526
44118CB00013B/1734